Your Ama
Commur
Your Te

G000136909

15 Essential Steps to creating a better relationship with your teen.

When their child reaches teenage years many parents struggle with adjusting to the new changes in their son or daughter. To say the least, communication becomes difficult. This book gives strategies to help parents feel more equipped for the task of navigating those years.

Questions parents ask:

- What do I do when my teen won't listen to me?
- How do I handle teen attitude?
- How do I set limits without fighting?
- What can I do to help my teen with peer pressure?

If communicating with your teen interests you, pick up a copy of this powerful fact-filled book today!

Very helpful little book. Being a parent you need information quick, succinct and immediate. This book delivers on all three,
Amazon Customer

The tips in this book would have improved my family's communication a great deal.
Carol P.

Brilliant guidance for parents, educators and therapists! A must read….
Laurie Hacking

Handy little book, great value, excellent advice
Sunil Cherian

This book is a life saver. Thank you Author Christine Alisa for your stress relief insights on dealing with y teem!!
Amazon Customer

Your Amazing
Itty Bitty®

Communicating
With Your Teenager
Book

*15 Simple Steps to creating a better
relationship with your teen*

Christine Alisa, MS

Published by Itty Bitty® Publishing
A subsidiary of S & P Productions, Inc.

Printed in the United States of America

Itty Bitty™ Publishing
311 Main Street, Suite E
El Segundo, CA 90245
(310) 640-8885

ISBN: 978-1-931191-67-8

*I dedicate this book to my daughter, Brianna,
whose love has brought me so much joy.*

Stop by our the Itty Bitty® website to find interesting blog entries regarding Communicating With Your Teenager.

www.IttyBittyPublishing.com

Or visit Christine Alisa, M.S. at:
www.PeaceThroughMetamorphosis.com

Email: chris@christinealisa.com

Table of Contents

Simple Steps

Step 1
Avoid Power Struggles

In this Itty Bitty Book you will find 15 simple things you can do to communicate successfully with your teenager. It is time to change the dialog and here is how you start.

1. Power struggles don't work.
2. Trying to get your point across only makes teens argue more fiercely.
3. You can't win. Teens have more energy and persistence.
4. Teens fight for control because they often feel powerless themselves.
5. Instead of arguing - stop! Leave the room.
6. Pick up the conversation later when you have 'cooled down.'
7. Identify how you feel. Frustrated? Angry? Hurt?
8. Breathe and share your feelings with a friend.

Change the conversation so your teen feels heard and respected.

- Find a neutral place to talk like the car.
- Be open, honest and non-judgmental.
- Express your own feelings: "I felt frustrated when we argued yesterday."
- Reflect your teen's feelings. "It must be frustrating for you when I ask you to clean your room."
- Listen to your teen, even if you disagree.
- He/she might say, "Yeah, you make me clean my room when I already have too much to do."
- Answer him/her with, "Yes, you are already overwhelmed and it felt like I made it worse."

Step 2
Unplug Your Buttons

We all have buttons, things that really bother us. Teenagers have a kind of 'radar' that can sense those buttons. Here are some tips to be aware of so you don't explode.

1. Verbal buttons like "You NEVER let me do what I want." Or "You ALWAYS pick on me."
2. Non-verbal buttons like the ATTITUDE of your teen.
3. BEHAVIORS like leaving his/her homework to the last minute.
4. Stop defending yourself or your position.
5. Don't respond with sarcasm or anger; then they 'got you.'
6. Think about what might be going on with your teen.
7. Your teen wants your attention, but often gets it in a negative way.
8. If you give your power away you lose control.

Tips to Avoid Getting Your Buttons Pushed:

- Before you react, breathe.
- Put the issue back on your teen like, "Something is going on with you, what is it?"
- Change the energy between the two of you by suggesting you plan something together. It could be just getting a coffee or an ice cream.
- Set aside time for yourself. Recharge your batteries.
- Give yourself some slack. Parenting teens is exhausting.
- Refrain from criticizing yourself if you 'lose it.' Just pick yourself up and start all over again.

Step 3
"What Happened To My Child and Who Is This Person I Am Living With?"

All of a sudden your child has morphed into another person with a different set of values and language. You feel confused and disoriented. However, once you understand them, they tend to change how they talk to you. Here are some ideas to start learning how to relate to your teen.

1. Remember your own teenage years; the differences and the similarities.
2. Puberty can cause a sense of imbalance and self-consciousness.
3. They love having more freedom but don't always know how to handle it.
4. Worries about 'fitting in' are highly important to them.
5. Comparing themselves to other peers is natural, but creates self-doubt.
6. They have many pressures at school, at sports or afterschool activities.
7. They need time to just collapse in order to regenerate.
8. Teens need more understanding than little children, since they don't understand themselves.

Tips to Understanding Your Teen

- Give him/her positive feedback regarding his/her strengths/gifts.
- Guide them, but don't give advice or lectures.
- Let them have their own opinions, even if you disagree.
- When your teen shuts down and won't talk, it can mean they just need their space, but it could also mean something is going on inside of them.
- Don't be afraid to ask gently what is going on with them. You might need to guess. Even if you are wrong, it still starts the conversation.
- Listen to them.
- Be authentic with your feelings and model for them how to express themselves.
- Moods will come and go. Depend on it.

Step 4
Be Clear About Your Limits

Communication will go much better with your teen if your limits are clear. Rules for teenagers are different from childhood, but teenagers tend to break them more often. Here are some points to consider when setting your limits with teens.

1. Be very specific about basic rules that are non-negotiable, such as when to be home at night or what kind of grades you expect; your values.
2. Clearly state the consequences if they break those rules.
3. Stay consistent with those rules and consequences.
4. Establish your limits with things like time on social media, phone or gaming.
5. Do not fall into the trap of manipulation from your teen.
6. Your teen needs reasonable structure from you because they are having trouble with their own internal limits.
7. On lesser limits (negotiable), try to listen to your teen and see if you feel comfortable loosening those limits for special circumstances.

What to Do When Teens Break the Rules:

- It is time to sit down and discuss what happened.
- Refrain from blaming, yelling or criticizing them.
- If it's a negotiable rule, ask your teen what they think would be a good consequence.
- Come up with an agreement between both of you as to a consequence.
- Your teen will feel more empowered and less likely to 'push' as often, if you give him/her a voice in the solution.
- Refrain from using the same consequence repeatedly, like grounding or taking things away.
- If it is a serious rule (non-negotiable) that has been broken, it is time for a serious talk or consulting a counselor.

Step 5
Keep it Light

Sometimes communication with teens can be light and easy, which puts your teen in a more responsive mood.

1. Pick a neutral time and location to talk.
2. Keep your mood light.
3. Use humor if it is not pointed at anyone or laugh at yourself. They love it when adults make mistakes.
4. Be 'up' on a subject that is current in their life like the day the All Star Team is going to get picked.
5. Notice if there has been a change in who they are hanging out with. Use that to talk.
6. Ask them if anybody said anything funny today.
7. Do not ask a lot of questions.
8. "Playing" with your teen helps him/her feel loved. Being silly or finding the humor in a situation is good for both of you.

Creative, short, light conversation ideas like these add more lightness:

- "I saw you hanging out with Ben. Are you friends again? You were both so funny when he was around more."
- "I can't believe I forgot when the tryouts are for the team. I think I need a new brain. Do you think there is hope for me?"
- "I'd love to hear who you are going to the dance with, please, please. I promise to keep it a secret."
- "You have been in your room all week unless you're eating with us. Can you come out a little more? I know you love it in there but I miss you."
- "I hear that teacher you have for Computer class is really funny. Did he say anything funny today?"
- "I love it when you tell me jokes. Heard any good ones?"

Step 6
Active Listening

An element of talking WITH your teen, not AT him/her is called active listening. It will do more for your communication with your teen than anything else. Here is how it works:

1. HEAR the feelings of your teen.
2. While your teen is talking, listen to what's "underneath"; in other words, what they are actually saying.
3. Think of a feeling that best reflects what you heard.
4. Identify the thoughts that come with the feeling.
5. Reflect those thoughts in your words.
6. Put the feeling word and the thought together and respond to your teen.
7. Acknowledge their response by putting another feeling word and thought together.
8. IMPORTANT: If your teen's feelings are not expressed, he/she will have trouble "thinking out problems."

Examples of active listening dialog with feelings and thoughts:

- Parent: "It seems like something is frustrating you."
- Teen: "I don't want to talk about it."
- Parent: "So, it feels like talking about it won't help."
- Teen: "No, it won't. Nothing will."
- Parent: "That must feel awful."
- Teen: "I said I don't want to talk about it."
- Parent: "I see. You feel like it is something impossible to fix."
- Teen: "Yeah, it is all over the school now that Rob is my boyfriend. I thought Nicki was my friend. She told everybody."
- Parent: "Nothing hurts more than a friend that does something like that."

Step 7
List of Feeling Words

The list provided is to help you best describe the feeling portion of Active Listening Skills. Practice using different ones to make your listening more impactful.

1. ANGRY, irritated, annoyed, furious.
2. SAD, discouraged, gloomy, unhappy.
3. CONFUSED, unsure, overwhelmed, shaken up, uncertain.
4. HAPPY, cheerful, pleased, delighted.
5. CAPABLE, able, prepared, competent.
6. CONCERNED, bothered, worried, pressured, anxious.
7. EXCITED, ecstatic, thrilled.
8. REJECTED, alone, cast off, left out, ignored, distant.
9. HOPELESS, helpless, discouraged, powerless, unsafe, insecure.
10. DEGRADED, insulted, laughed at, put down, insulted.
11. GUILTY, blamed, accused, burdened.

'Feeling Descriptors'

Other possibilities to utilize when using active listening instead of feeling words:

- "You feel like you have a dark cloud hanging over your head."
- "Your world has exploded with excitement."
- "The pressure never ends."
- "You feel like the world is out to get you."
- "You can't stop jumping up and down inside for joy."
- "You feel like your feet are stuck in mud."
- "The sadness is weighing you down."
- "It feels like no one understands you at all."

Step 8
Drug and/or Alcohol Abuse

Some preliminary guidelines to keep in mind when discussing difficult issues like substance use/abuse by your teen are:

1. Watch for the signs. Sudden changes in behavior or habits, secretive behavior, lying, a drop in grades.
2. Tell your teen firmly, but gently that you need to talk.
3. Be direct about what you have noticed.
4. Listen and try to go deeper into what is driving that behavior. It is really a symptom of something else.
5. Try to discover the deeper reasons that caused them to use/abuse.
6. Expect that they will be defensive, angry or shut down.
7. Explore teen groups in your area that help kids within AA or NA, or take him/her to a counselor.
8. If substance abuse is practiced in the family, it is time to get outside help with no shame.

Other Things to Keep in Mind When Talking to Your Teen about Substance Abuse:

- When a show comes on TV, use it as a platform for a short discussion on drugs.
- If you catch your teen using, ask what drove him/her to use in the first place.
- Pay more attention to your teen. Who is he/she hanging out with and where? Who are the parents of those kids?
- Do not use threats or blame.
- Try not to overreact; stay as calm as possible.
- If they shut down, express how you feel.
- Talk to other parents or groups for support.

Step 9
Teen Attitude

All teens show you attitude at one time or another. Learning to react in a healthy way opens up the path for better communication.

1. When teens show attitude they are not connecting with you - they are blowing you off.
2. Attitude is a way they have of defending themselves and staying non-committal.
3. Do you feel shut out, angry or frustrated with their attitude?
4. Tell your teen what you feel like when they show you attitude.
5. Ask them what is going on.
6. If you get the "whatever" comeback, do not react.
7. Tell them you need their help in the conversation. It can't be just one-sided.
8. Don't push. Wait for an opening, but don't wait too long.

More Tips to Help with Teen Attitude:

- Don't let their attitude stop you from communicating.
- Try to guess at what is going on in their life.
- Ask, "You seem unhappy about something. Can you tell me about it?"
- The attitude may mean ANGER. Ask them if something made them angry.
- If they are angry at you for something, be prepared to listen and be honest about your part.
- Teens are testing all the time. Attitude is a test.
- They want to know your boundaries/limits/what you will allow.

Step 10
Developmental Stages in Teens

The teen years are typically 13 – 18 years old and there are significant differences within that range. It seems that many teens are maturing earlier these days, so I will include age 12 as well. Here are some of the characteristics:

Age 12-14:

1. They are going through transitions with their body, mind and personality.
2. The need to have alone time is important to assimilate these new experiences.
3. Can be moody; want less time with family and more with peers.
4. Body image becomes almost obsessive in nature.
5. Worry and confusion takes over in many areas as he/she is looking for a new identity.
6. Group activities and socializing with peers and opposite sex highly important.
7. Teens want independence from parents, but use fighting with their parents as a way to make contact.

Developmental Stages in Teens (continued):

Age 15-16

- Rebellious behavior against authority occurs.
- Holding in feelings or covering them up is tied to not wanting to be seen as weak.
- More self-reliant.
- Can be extremely uncommunicative with parents. Often occurs with boys.
- More maturity and critical thinking abilities.
- Debate their opinions with others.
- These years can be a crossroads for teens; whether to stay in school or drop out or get totally caught up in school and group activities.

Age 17-18

- More of a sense of self and role in life.
- If their self-confidence is low, discovering their role in the world can pose problems.
- Exploring more long-term relationships outside of the family.
- More intimacy with others; i.e. sharing of feelings.

Step 11
Episodes

All teens go through periods of moodiness. It is normal. Knowing how to 'read' your teen's episodes and knowing when to 'leave them alone' are critical skills for a parent or guardian. Here are some tips:

1. Allow your teen time for quiet, introspective moods: "I just want to be by myself."
2. Hyper-moods are common. Teens have a lot of energy.
3. Moods that continue for days are not moods, but indicators of depression or anxiety, so pay attention.
4. Mood swings are common, but if in extreme, sit down and talk to your teen.
5. A sudden mood change can indicate something has happened. Again, talk to your teen.
6. A non-communicative mood is common in some teens, especially boys.
7. Sometimes mood swings can be the result of substance abuse.

What To Do With Emotional Episodes
Like Mood Swings and Depressive Moods:

- Take it seriously, but do not lecture.
- You can say, "I am frustrated when I see that you look sad and I don't know what to do about it."
- Or, "It scares me sometimes when you won't open up and seem so down. I wish you would talk to me. Maybe we can work it out together."
- Or, "I have noticed that you don't seem happy lately. Did something happen?"
- Listen to your teen. Just the act of listening to the reason they are in a 'mood,' lessens the intensity and provides a 'sounding board.'

Step 12
The Manipulation Trap

Teens manipulate to get what they want, or to avoid getting into trouble. Staying out of their trap can be a full-time job. Here are some suggestions to avoid the trap.

1. As much as possible be prepared with your limits.
2. Clearly state your expectations. "The allowance I gave you is enough for the week. I expect you to use it wisely."
3. Give two choices: "You can go to the party wearing what I say is okay or you can skip the party."
4. Teens will push to get what they want. It is their job. They need to find your limits. Expect it.
5. When they seem to have manipulated a situation to their favor, sit down and listen carefully. There may be more to it.
6. Work together with your teen to problem-solve a situation

Tips to Avoid Being Manipulated

- Instead of going against your better judgment, redirect.
- Example: Teen: "You gotta let me go to Carly's overnight party."
- Parent: "I wish I could say yes, however you haven't finished your homework like you said you would."
- Teen: "I'll do it later. I promise."
- Parent: "That's what you've said before."
- Teen: "Everyone is going. They will call me dumb if I don't go."
- Parent: "I know you really want to go and I bet you wished you had finished your homework so you could go."
- Put the responsibility back on your teen by redirecting without blaming or dismissing their feelings.

Step 13
Peer Pressure

All teens feel a need to belong to a group. They go along with the group and want to conform, and their self-esteem is tied to it. You can help your teen by talking about this important part of their life.

1. Girls tend to want to talk about their friends and the 'drama' that goes on between them.
2. Boys tend not to talk about their friends, but that doesn't mean they don't need to.
3. Girls do not want your advice, but they do want you to 'hear' about the problems.
4. Boys may need to you to encourage them to talk.
5. Role-play with your teen in positive ways to respond to the pressure from others; i.e. you be your teen and your teen canbe the 'friend applying pressure.'
6. Reverse roles and practice different assertive responses; i.e. "Yeah, we're friends, but I don't agree about how you treated Bill the other day."
7. Re-enforce that your teen is allowed to have feelings and opinions.

Peer Bullying: How to Help Your Teen

- Bullying is on the rise. One out of five teens up to 15 yrs. old participates in cyber bullying.
- Watch for signs in your teen; such as any changes in their self-esteem.
- If your teen is a victim of bullying, contact the parent of the bully, as well as school authorities. Be proactive.
- Check their Social Media activity, phone/ texting.
- Teens that bully want to feel the power it gives them.
- When your teen 'puts down' others, tell them, "It offends me when I hear you talk about someone that way."
- Start a conversation about bullying. Watch how they react and use active listening.
- Remember to praise their positive attitudes and behaviors to build their self-esteem.

Step 14
The Better You Are,
The Better Your Teen Will Be

Raising teenagers requires fortitude, patience and energy. The teen years are comparable to the toddler years. They want independence, but parents are scared for their safety. Taking care of yourself will benefit your relationship with your teen. Here are some ideas for self care:

1. Expect that your teen will want distance from you. Don't feel hurt.
2. Spend time doing nourishing things for yourself. Don't forget about yourself.
3. Find outlets for your own emotions. Exercising, screaming in the car with the windows closed, writing in a journal or talking to a good friend.
4. Be creative. Use the interests of your teen to match with your own.
5. Suggest activities that have nothing to do with your parental role, like playing board games with your teen (their choice, then your choice). Take turns.
6. Remember: This too will pass.
7. Parents, work together to support one another. Have each other's back in a fortified front.

More Ideas to Consider for Self-care:

- Be authentic and truthful with yourself.
- When you are honest about your own limits, feelings or behaviors, you model those for your teen.
- Find calming activities such as meditation, yoga, martial arts, being in nature.
- Give yourself a break. Take these suggestions if they feel like a good fit for you. Do not overwhelm yourself.
- Do something different.
- Expect to make mistakes. It is part of the learning process.
- Seek out therapy for yourself.

Step 15
Outside Help

Sometimes it is necessary to seek a counselor/
therapist or parenting group. Here are some
guidelines to follow:

1. If your teen is not responding to your
   repeated attempts to communicate, do not
   hesitate to find help.
2. It takes a 'village' to raise a child and
   parents do not know all the answers.
3. If there are serious issues like substance
   abuse, sexual, physical or emotional
   abuse, seek out a qualified therapist.
4. Taking a parenting class helps in feeling
   more confident in talking to your teen.
5. Develop a support system, i.e. family,
   trusted friends or a group.
6. If there is a divorce, teens may need to
   talk to someone else because they are
   afraid to hurt one or both parents.
7. If your teen shows signs of 'cutting,'
   eating disorders, severe acting out, failing
   in school or depression, seek outside
   help.

Things to Consider When Finding a Therapist:

- Interview the therapist on the phone or in person before starting therapy.
- Often a recommendation from someone you trust is a good start.
- Ask about the therapist's background and therapeutic techniques.
- Make sure you feel comfortable with the therapist. Use your intuition.
- Ask if they specialize with teens and their families.
- Talk to your teen and say, "I feel that I need help in talking to you, so I have found a therapist. It is the family's problem, not just you. I want us to be happier and healthier."
- After the first session, ask your teen what he/she thought of the therapist.
- Follow the therapist's guidelines.

You've finished. Before you go...

Tweet/share that you finished this book.

Please star rate this book.

Reviews are solid gold to writers. Please take a few minutes to give us some itty bitty feedback on this book.

ABOUT THE AUTHOR

My love for children and teenagers began when I was a teacher, but I felt I could make a bigger difference with teens and their families by becoming a counselor. For over 25 years as a Marriage Family Therapist, I have helped teens and their families overcome the roadblocks and misunderstandings that get in the way of their happiness and closeness.

I have written this book for parents and guardians who struggle with the changes they see in their teenager and feel helpless to know how to deal with them. I want adults to be empowered; to have strategies and tools for communication as their child enters this phase of his/her life.

My other passion is the trainings I conduct with therapists internationally. I help them use the therapeutic techniques that I have developed to help understand children and adolescents more deeply.

I have specialized in working with children and adolescents in areas of trauma, abuse, anger issues, learning disabilities, ADD and ADHD in my private practice in Southern California.

Please visit Christine Alisa, M.S. at:
www.PeaceThroughMetamorphosis.com

Email: chris@christinealisa.com

If You Liked This Book You Might Also Enjoy

* **Your Amazing Itty Bitty® Travel Planning Book** – Rosemary Workman

* **Your Amazing Itty Bitty® Weight Loss Book** – Suzy Prudden and Joan-Meijer-Hirschland

* **Your Amazing Itty Bitty® Family Leadership Book** – Jacqueline Schaeffer

With many more Amazing Itty Bitty® Books to available in paperback and online…

Printed in Great Britain
by Amazon

62185590R00031